1,003
Great Things
About
Friends

Other Books by Lisa Birnbach
1,003 Great Things About Kids
1,003 Great Things About Getting Older
The Official Preppy Handbook
Lisa Birnbach College Books
Going to Work
Loose Lips

Other Books by Ann Hodgman
1,003 Great Things About Kids
1,003 Great Things About Getting Older
My Baby-sitter Is a Vampire (series)
Stinky Stanley (series)
Beat This!
Beat That!

Other Books by Patricia Marx
1,003 Great Things About Kids
1,003 Great Things About Getting Older
How to Regain Your Virginity
You Can Never Go Wrong by Lying
Blockbuster
Now Everybody Really Hates Me
Now I Will Never Leave the Dinner Table
How to Survive Junior High
Meet My Staff

1,003 Great Things About Friends

Lisa Birnbach • Ann Hodgman • Patricia Marx

**Andrews McMeel
Publishing**

Kansas City

www.andrewsmcmeel.com

02 03 BIN 10 9 8 7 6 5

Library of Congress Cataloging-in-Publication Data
Birnbach, Lisa.
    1,003 great things about friends / Lisa Birnbach,
Ann Hodgman, Patricia Marx.
      p. cm.
  ISBN 0-7407-0021-9 (pbk.)
  1. Friendship Humor. I. Hodgman, Ann. II. Marx,
Patricia (Patricia A.) III. Title. IV. Title: One thousand
three great things about friends
    PN6231.F748 B57 1999
    818'.5402—dc21   99-21530
                                                       CIP

Book design by Lisa Martin

ATTENTION: SCHOOLS AND BUSINESSES

Andrews McMeel books are available at quantity discounts with bulk purchase for educational, business, or sales promotional use. For information, please write to: Special Sales Department, Andrews McMeel Publishing, 4520 Main Street, Kansas City, Missouri 64111.

1,003
Great Things
About Friends

∽

You hate the same people.

∽

A friend will tell you the
truth about whether those
pants make you look fat.

A friend will lie about whether those pants make you look fat.

☙

You always have someone to complain to.

☙

She'll tell you, "Go ahead and eat all of the cookies before they cool down."

You can wear your worst
clothes around a friend.

∽

You could be dumped in the middle
of the Sahara Desert with sand
blowing into your eyes and dusk
falling—but you'd still recognize
your best friend's handwriting.

∽

If you tell a friend a secret,
she will keep the secret by telling
only one other person.

Friends don't mind
when you call and
wake them up.

It's not much fun to toast
marshmallows alone.

Friends don't bite.

You don't care if a
friend hears you going
to the bathroom.

∽

You're not obliged to say
"Fine" when a friend asks
how you are.

∽

Someone to split
the bagel with.

Dumb Questions You Can Ask a Friend

∽

"How much is this sweater
in dollars?"

∽

"Does the knife face
out or in?"

"What's an integer?"

"Is Gerald Ford dead?"

"Which is my given name and which is my surname?"

"Is Milan in Spain?"

"Can you make a
left on red?"

∽

"Is it 'fall forward,
spring back' or 'spring
forward, fall back'?"

∽

"How many days are there
in February?"

"How many judges are
there on the Supreme
Court, anyway?"

"What does *sui
generis* mean?"

Someone to thank at
the Grammys.

You're not liable when
they go bankrupt.

A professional
bra stuffer.

No need to spend
Thanksgiving with them.

❦

She'll tell your parents you
drank only virgin piña coladas
at the party last night.

❦

Now you have numbers
you can add to your
speed-dial function.

They'll take your kids to
stand outside *The Today Show*
at six A.M. in a record-breaking
cold wave. In a novelty hat,
carrying a silly sign.

෧

You can return the birthday
present your friend gave you
without hurting her feelings.

෧

Cancel dinner plans
with impunity.

Without friends, your address
book would be blank.

∾

A friend sides with you,
no matter what the law says.

∾

Their gossip tolerance level
is the same as yours.

Good Friends
Take Turns

∽

If you read the articles
about Ireland, I'll read the
ones about Kosovo.

∽

You get to rent *Spice World*
today if I get to rent
Clueless tomorrow.

I'll wear the Oscar de la Renta
to the hospital ball and you
can wear it to the Stewarts'
anniversary party.

∽

I'll do car pool for a
month if you make
the costumes.

∽

I'll ask for directions
if you'll pump the gas.

I'll get extra dressing on the side
if you give me your fries.

᠅

I'll give you all my Milk Duds if
you give me all your Sweetarts.

᠅

You get out and push; I'll steer.

᠅

No, *you* get out and push;
I'll steer.

Someone to pull an
all-nighter with.

~

She knows the head of
the nursery school and will
call her for you.

~

A friend will lend you
the car even if you don't
have a driver's license.

Her clothes are
your clothes.

༄

Someone to spend
Easter break with you so
you don't have to go home.

༄

A friend is allowed to
feed your dog from the table even
though no one else can.

Someone to drive
with you all night
to L. L. Bean.

∽

Will never forget your
definitive portrayal of:
• Fairy Number 1
in *Midsummer-Night's Dream*
in third grade
• Sancho Panza in ninth grade
• Elizabeth Proctor in twelfth grade

Friends in the building
will get your name to the top
of the list for a condo.

❧

It's fine to stand in
the kitchen throughout your
entire meal together.

❧

Doesn't think you need a
shrink. Just come out for the
weekend and *relax!*

A Cyrano-like phone caller
whenever you need one.

∽

According to one theory,
kids who fight with their parents
a lot are apt to have more friends
than kids who don't.

∽

Listen, he didn't really mean
what he said that time.

A Friend in Need Is a Friend . . .

∾

. . . in dire financial straits

∾

. . . whose phone calls you
don't want to return

∾

. . . who owes you one

. . . named Tanya Tucker

∽

. . . with a barn that
needs raising

∽

. . . who knows you have
a swimming pool

∽

. . . who's moving into a
new apartment

. . . who's afraid to pick up
dead bugs herself

∽

. . . whose parents are in town,
and he wants to give a dinner
party in their honor

∽

. . . whose fax machine is
broken, and you have one

. . . who knows your
father is hiring a new
product manager

. . . who wants to
"borrow" your most
reliable babysitter

A friendship is
less likely to break up
than a marriage.

❧

Chances are, your friend
has some friends you
can appropriate.

❧

They know your cast
of characters.

When you're eating with
a friend, you don't need any
conveyance for the onion dip.

∽

In a real emergency, she'll lend you
her husband (unless you remind
everyone of Pamela Harriman).

∽

Friendship means never
having to say you're sorry—
no, wait, that's love.

Knows the day you
got pregnant.

❧

Knows you're pregnant
before you do.

❧

Your friend has seen
you at all your weights . . .
and still likes you.

You don't have to bring a house
present when you visit.

Someone to sell pecans to for
the alumnae association.

More fiercely vigilant
than you when it comes to
personal slights against you.

Skip the thank-you notes.

∾

Someone to glop on your
henna paste/hair color/sunless
suntan lotion.

∾

"You can make up after a fight."
—Laurie McCall, age 6

You can count on them to hide the incriminating evidence in your house if you die suddenly.

∽

Your friend will tell you the truth about your new hair color.

∽

At your wedding, your friend will talk to your great-uncle about his cataract operation so no one else has to.

Great Things
About Growing Up
with Friends

∾

Age 1 day) Bonding in the
hospital nursery.

∾

Age 1 week) It's not a
social solecism to burp in
front of your friends.

Age 1 month) At last
s/he can smile at you!

∽

Age 1) You're not expected
to notice the other babies
in your play group.

∽

Age 2) You're not expected to
share with the other toddlers
in your play group.

Age 3) Most of your
friends no longer throw
sand in your eyes.

∽

Age 4) Perfectly
acceptable to use the
toilet while your friend
stands next to you,
watching.

Age 5) You know *way* more
of the alphabet than many
of your friends.

Age 6) Someone to
protect you from the
second graders.

Age 7) She'll let you
style her hair.

Age 8) If your mom says, "Will you come in here a minute, please?" in a threatening voice, you can make your friend come with you. And when your friend goes home, you can "confess" that it was really the friend who broke your mother's priceless heirloom.

∽

Age 9) Your best friend doesn't mind that you both have a crush on the same kid.

Age 10) When you have a fight with your best friend, you can still walk to school together—just on opposite sides of the street.

∽

Age 11) He won't make fun of you when you fall off your skateboard.

∽

Age 12) Or laugh at you when you start to "develop."

Age 13) Lots of bar and
bat mitzvah parties.

∽

Age 14) Someone usually
has an older sibling who
will drive you places.

∽

Age 15) You can call
your friend's parents by
their first names.

Age 16) Now you don't
need a friend with an
older sibling who will drive
you places. All you need
is a friend with a car.

&

Age 17) Someone to
spend the whole evening
in the bathroom with you
at the senior prom.

Age 18) Someone who'll vote for the candidate of your choice.

∽

Age 19) Finally someone who can introduce you to college guys.

∽

Age 20) S/he actually likes to listen to your stupid philosophies.

∽

Age 21) Mourn your lost childhood together.

You can ask a friend
the difference between the
IRA and the Irish Republic
without feeling stupid.

೫

A free babysitter
for your kids.

೫

No need to exchange
Christmas presents.

They will give you
a loan at a much better
rate than the bank.

❧

Will help you search
for split ends.

❧

You can call a friend
up on a Saturday night and
ask her to the movies that
very same night.

She feels the same
degree of loyalty to the British
monarchy that you do.

❧

A friend can get
your dad a private room
in the hospital.

❧

Eat out of her refrigerator
with no invitation.

Unlimited supply of her
feminine hygiene products.

ᔕ

Long car rides
without talking.

ᔕ

A friend purports not
to mind if you break a date
with her for someone you
have a crush on.

Someone you can sneak
out of the office and go to
Loehmann's with.

∽

You don't have to look up
their phone numbers.

∽

You and your friend
find the same boring
things fascinating.

A Friend in the
Past Could . . .

∾

. . . fasten your corset
strings for you

∾

. . . take your place in
the guillotine

46

. . . bury you when you
die from the plague

❧

. . . help you bind your feet

❧

. . . help dig those big rocks
out of your field

❧

. . . get you a seat on the ark
when it starts raining

. . . invent the telephone and
then call you up

ᕲ

. . . bring you dress goods
from the country store

ᕲ

. . . fetch the doctor when
you're birthin'

. . . vouch for your not
being a witch

∾

. . . sing songs about the old
country with you

∾

. . . help you forge
identity papers to smuggle
you out of the country

. . . invite you to the ball
at the squire's mansion

∾

. . . club the saber-toothed tiger
who's about to attack you

∾

. . . help you pan
for gold out west

. . . give you the best
gossip at the quilting bee

ꕥ

. . . get you tickets
to the first Olympics

ꕥ

. . . prevent you from
looking behind you and
turning into a pillar of salt

A real friend will
visit you in jail.

∽

After a ten-year break
with a friend, you can pick
up right where you left off—
talking about Matt Seidman.

∽

She can teach you
how to inhale.

Someone to wake you
up when you fall asleep
in the library.

"Friend shorthand."

"My best" just goes with friend.

"My best shoes" doesn't have
the same wallop.

Someone who remembers
what you looked like with
your old nose, but would
never remind you of it.

∽

A reason to pay attention
to those endless solicitations from
long-distance phone companies.

∽

Sometimes your friend has
a husband who can come over
and fix your storm windows.

Your wife's friends will
have you over for dinner when
she goes out of town.

∽

Your friend will tell you
if your fly's unzipped.

∽

Your friend will tell
you if you have lipstick
on your teeth.

Someone to stalk your
ex for you.

∾

Friends are better at
cheering you up than
parents are.

∾

Won't laugh at you for
misunderstanding sexual terms
when you first hear them.

Someone to tell you
without cruelty that those
Capri pants really do emphasize
your hips and that you looked so
good in the brown leggings.

∽

And those brown leggings
would look great with that velvet
tunic you got last fall.

∽

No makeup is necessary
when you're together.

Nice Reasons Friends Can't be Trusted

∽

He always pays more
than his share.

∽

She might be giving you
a surprise party.

She never wants to hurt
your feelings.

∽

He knows you have
high blood pressure.

∽

Because your pastor told
him not to tell you.

A friend will write college
recommendations for your son,
even when your son got kicked out
of high school for hacking into
the school's computer system.

∽

The ship that never sinks.

∽

Kegger!

You can always stay
with a friend's family when
you're traveling.

∽

Someone to share the
driving with.

∽

It's (sort of) okay for you to
yell at a friend's kids.

Without friends,
Friendly's ice cream shop
would just be Ly's.

∽

She won't tell anyone
you eat entire cans
of frosting.

∽

If you split up with a friend,
you don't have to pay alimony.

According to a recent survey,
people are less likely to lie to their
friends than to their mothers.

∽

Can pick out just the video you
wanted to watch.

∽

Still envious of your
record/tape/CD collection.

A surrogate family.

Doesn't mind being
regifted at all.

A friend can tell you how
to get out of quicksand.

A friend will not shun you for
taking up smoking again.

She knows your menstrual
cycle better than you do.

∾

Starring in that community
theater production of *Our Town*?
You can count on at least one
person in the audience.

∾

Knows stuff about you that
you would never tell your spouse.
And neither would she.

65

No Friends?
In a Pinch, You
Can Substitute . . .

❧

mortgage officers

❧

car salespeople

❧

dental hygienists

phone solicitors

∽

siblings

∽

parents

∽

bra-fitting salesladies

∽

editors

people who talk to you
in the elevator

❧

funeral directors

❧

your waitress

❧

journalists

people who all you
know about them is their
e-mail addresses

checkout ladies
at the library

your college classmate
on the fund-raising
committee

your personal trainer

∽

a psychoanalyst

∽

the people who live down
the hall, even though
you never see them

∽

your next-door neighbor
(if you need a cup of sugar)

a taxi driver

ɕ

your OB-GYN

ɕ

the other clients at
Overeaters Anonymous

Going down the slide isn't
much fun alone.

෨

Going to an amusement park
really isn't fun alone.

෨

Singing "One Hundred Bottles
of Beer on the Wall"
is pointless alone.

Someone to quickly
improvise a solution when
you split your pants.

∽

A really good friend will risk her
life for you—so if the two of you
find yourselves being hijacked
together, you're in luck!

∽

With a friend, you don't have
to wait for the food to get hot or
cold before you start eating.

Who else would call your boss and pretend to be your doctor, saying you can't come in to work because you have a medical emergency?

❧

A friend will remember what you gave her for her last birthday.

❧

Or forget, if you accidentally give her the same thing again.

Someone to go to the
infirmary with.

∽

A friend is more willing than a
doctor to give you free samples of
Valium and diet pills.

∽

Just hearing a friend's voice
makes you feel better.

A Useful Friend . . .

∽

Can identify birds

∽

Knows which caterer
is the best

∽

Always carries cough
drops, breath mints,
and extra stamps

Knows everything
about computers

Merges fearlessly onto
the expressway

Speaks Spanish fluently

Is a good proofreader

Knows how to fix a flat tire
(and has a jack)

∽

Knows how to start a dead
battery (and has jumper cables)

∽

Owns a generator when the
power lines are down

Knows how to forge your signature—no, wait a minute, that may be a little *too* useful

Is able to write medical prescriptions

Has lots of transferable frequent flier miles

Loves to give parties

᠄

Wears your size

᠄

Can answer all etiquette
questions

᠄

Runs a dating service

Owns a telephone with the
capability to make conference calls

∽

Knows where all the public
bathrooms are

∽

Always has quarters for the
parking meter

∽

Answers to the name "Mommy"

A friend would go to the
five A.M. opening of the great
antique show, outside, in
the winter, in the rain.

∽

Still thinks of you admiringly as
"the babe from Reid Hall."

∽

She'll keep track of
your living will.

If you witness an alien invasion, no
one will believe you unless a friend was
there to corroborate your story.

∽

A friend can get you to
the captain's table.

∽

If a friend says it's okay to miss
the deadline for renewing your
driver's license, you can blame that
friend when you get caught with
an expired license.

You could be brainwashed by the enemy as a POW, but you'd still remember your best friend's phone number.

~

Go ahead—start with dessert.

~

In horror movies, it's usually the friend who gets killed, not the star.

~

Someone to tell your spouse what you really want for Christmas.

Keeps a pair of shoes in
your size at her house.

∽

When a friend says, "Can I give
you a hand with that?" she won't
get mad if you say yes.

∽

Shares your daily concern for the
girls in *Apartment 3-G.*

A Useless Friend . . .

∽

Kleptomaniac

∽

Sex addict

∽

Knows no doctors socially

∽

Lives too far away

A Useless Friend . . .

Has a horrible spouse

❧

Has "stomach problems"

❧

Works for Donna Karan but
won't get you the discount

❧

"Forgot my wallet again"

❧

Always tells the truth

Having friends protects you from being one of those loners who turn into mass murderers.

∽

A friend who dresses better than you do will improve your standards.

∽

A friend who dresses more sloppily than you is someone you can relax around.

It is statistically likely that a friend who is a braggart feels insecure around you.

It's okay to put your feet on a friend's sofa even if you're wearing shoes.

Someone to tell you which Darin is Dick York and which is the other guy.

She, too, remembers wanting to
be just like Patty Duke.

❧

She'll tell you when it's time to
get rid of the comb-over.

❧

He'll tell you when it's time to
get rid of the Cleopatra-style
black eyeliner.

You probably don't have any
friends who are vampires.

⌇

Friends don't let politics
get in the way.

⌇

When you visit for the weekend,
a friend will stock her house
with your favorite soda even
though she never drinks soda.

A friend will tell you
secrets she's been sworn
to silence about.

Aren't you glad you're
both over your
horse-riding phase?

Some friends keep
dishes/candy in their
living room.

Likes to swim in the same
temperature water as you.

∽

Doesn't think you're a wuss for
turning around one vertical mile
from the summit of Mount Everest.

∽

Someone to prop you up if you're
singing in the first row at the
school concert and you faint and
start to slide off the bleachers.

Great Things Great People Said to (or About) Friends

∾

"I should have written you a longer letter, but it is my unhappy fate seldom to treat people as they deserve."

—Jane Austen

"I can scarcely bid you good bye, even in a letter. I always made an awkward bow. God bless you!"

—*Keats's last letter,
to Charles Armitage Brown*

∽

"I desire so to conduct the affairs of this administration that if at the end, when I come to lay down the reins of power, I have lost every other friend on earth, I shall at least have one friend left, and that friend shall be down inside me."

—*Abraham Lincoln*

"There is an old-time toast which
is golden for its beauty. 'When
you ascend the hill of prosperity,
may you not meet a friend.'"

—*Mark Twain*

∽

"The best mirror is an old friend."

—*George Herbert*

∽

"A friend cannot be known in
prosperity; and an enemy cannot
be hidden in adversity."

—*The Apocrypha*

"Friendship is Love
without his wings."
—*Lord Byron*

❧

"Forsake not an old friend;
for the new is not comparable
to him: a new friend is as new
wine; when it is old, thou shalt
drink it with pleasure."
—*The Apocrypha*

"I do then with my friends as I do
with my books. I would have
them where I can find them,
but I seldom use them."

—*Ralph Waldo Emerson*

∽

"I was angry with my friend:
I told my wrath, my wrath did end."

—*Blake*

∽

"A friend is, as it were,
a second self."

—*Cicero*

"The friendship that can cease
has never been real."

—*Saint Jerome*

∽

"If you have a friend worth loving,
Love him. Yes, and let him know
That you love him, ere life's evening
Tinge his brow with sunset glow.
Why should good words ne'er be said
Of a friend till he is dead?"

—*Daniel Webster Hoyt*

"Yes'm, old friends is always best, 'less you can catch a new one that's fit to make an old one out of."

—*Sarah Orne Jewett*

❧

"So long as we are loved by others, I would almost say that we are indispensable; and no man is useless while he has a friend."

—*Robert Louis Stevenson*

"One friend in a lifetime is much;
two are many; three are hardly
possible. Friendship needs a
certain parallelism of life, a
community of thought,
a rivalry of aim."
—*Henry Brooks Adams*

∽

"It is a true saying, that a man
must eat a peck of salt with his
friend, before he knows him."
—*Cervantes*

"Give me the avowed,
erect, and manly foe,
Firm I can meet,
perhaps return the blow;
But of all plagues, good Heaven,
thy wrath can send,
Save, save, oh save me from
the candid friend!"
—*George Canning*

∽

"What is a friend? A single soul
dwelling in two bodies."
—*Aristotle*

"To me, fair friend,
you never can be old,
For as you were when
first your eye I ey'd,
Such seems your beauty still."
—*Shakespeare*

∽

"Treat your friend as if he
might become an enemy."
—*Publilius Syrus*

"What though youth gave
us love and roses,
Age still leaves us friends and wine."
—*Thomas Moore*

∽

"He who has a thousand friends
has not a friend to spare."
—*Ali Ibn-Abu-Talib*

∽

"Friends have all things
in common."
—*Plato*

"I love everything that's old:
old friends, old times,
old manners, old books,
old wines."
—*Oliver Goldsmith*

∽

"Thrice blessed are our friends:
they come, they stay,
And presently they go away."
—*Richard R. Kirk*

"The cunning seldom
gain their ends;
The wise are never without friends."
—*Anonymous*

∽

"A man, sir, should keep his
friendship in a constant repair."
—*Samuel Johnson*

∽

"To like and dislike the same things,
that is indeed true friendship."
—*Sallust*

"An argument needs no reason,
nor a friendship."

—*Ibycus*

∽

"Friendship is a
sheltering tree."

—*Samuel Taylor Coleridge*

∽

"Time, which strengthens
friendship, weakens love."

—*Jean de La Bruyère*

"True friendship is never serene."

—*Madame de Sévigné*

∾

"What is the odds so long as
the fire of soul is kindled at
the taper of conwiviality,
and the wing of friendship
never moults a feather!"

—*Charles Dickens*

Knows all the lyrics to the *That Girl* theme song—not just the "gingham, bluebirds" line.

෨

Someone to tell you when it makes sense to try to get a stain out, and when not to bother.

෨

"No, really, you don't look anything like Penny Marshall."

Has the same level of tolerance,
or lack thereof, in regard to
horoscopes and crystals.

∽

Having a friend taking orders
next to you makes a fast-food
job almost tolerable.

∽

She'll take your books along when
she's going to the library.

Better than you at applying concealer to "problem breakouts."

෨

Having a friend who's cheating on her spouse lets you experience the thrill of an illicit affair vicariously.

෨

Having a wacky friend permits you to feel lofty.

She won't tell anyone you
were a transfer student.

❧

She's so self-absorbed she makes
you look like Mother Teresa.

❧

Go ahead—watch *Password*
together.

❧

You can sing in front of a friend.

Someone to do up that little
fastener thingy at the top of the
zipper on your dress.

ဢ

String-and-tin-can telephones.

ဢ

She'll pretend she can't
tell the difference between real
floor tile and vinyl.

Lies It's Okay to Tell a Friend

∽

"No, actually you look as if
you've *lost* weight."

∽

"You're not boring me."

∽

"That's what friends are for."

"Sure, I'd be happy to."

❧

"Honestly, no one noticed."

❧

"Your kids are so smart
and well behaved!"

❧

"Of course they're not too tight.
They look great."

"I've never heard anything
so unfair."

∽

"You're doing a great job.
Your boss is obviously insecure—
that's all."

∽

"With that complexion,
you don't *need* foundation."

"That scale always weighs
a little high."

∽

"Of course you're not
spoiling the baby."

∽

"You picked the perfect
fabric for this sofa."

∽

"What stain? I don't see
anything."

"With everything you've got going on, no wonder you don't have time to exercise."

∽

"No one expects you to be perfect."

∽

"Of course I don't mind. Why should you keep track of my birthday?"

"Why didn't I say you
had corn stuck in your teeth?
Because I didn't notice!"

∽

"I don't see any gray."

∽

"This is delicious."

∽

"I'm not sleeping with
your spouse."

She'll be sure to let you know
that your Carrie Donovan glasses
were a big mistake.

∽

Friends don't laugh when you
slip on an icy sidewalk—unless you
fall in a really hilarious way.

∽

In high school, friends are *very*
conscientious about letting you
know every single rumor anyone
ever starts about you.

Whoever heard of dusting the house before a friend comes over?

∽

Supports your divine right to your own phone line, even in the face of parental opposition.

∽

When you return to the buffet table for the third time, you can claim you're just getting food for a friend.

Someone to talk you into getting
your eyebrow pierced.

∽

The two of you can develop
a code for telling each other
when something is hanging
out of your nose.

∽

Someone who doesn't complain
about all those times you put your
name first on the reports you
did together at work.

Someone to remind you
who Mike Richter is.

❧

Who else would let you brush your
teeth and spit in their kitchen sink?

❧

You never need to put in your
contact lenses for a friend.

❧

Or take a shower.

123

Or get out of bed.

∽

A friend happily reads the Week
in Review and lets you have
the Sunday Style section.

∽

She'll let you have the first taxi.

∽

She'll wait with you until
your bus comes.

A friend will spot you in
gymnastics even if you haven't
shaved your legs.

❧

A friend will sit in
the smoking section with
you so you can smoke.

❧

Kind enough to lie and say
you're prettier now than you
were twenty years ago.

Very, Very Important Things Never to Do With a Friend

❧

Cohost a party.

❧

Coauthor a book.

Share a hotel room.

Go on a diet together.

Buy matching dresses.

Play Truth or Dare.

Drive cross-country.

Travel through Europe
on the cheap.

∽

Argue about a woman's
right to choose.

∽

Confess that you have a
crush on his/her father.

∽

Have sex just to see
what it's like.

She'll worry that you won't
get a parking space so you
can be the calm one.

∽

Go away with a friend when
you're fifty and get face-lifts.

∽

If she has an insider trading tip,
you'll be the first to know.

If there's an afterlife,
you'll know someone there.

❧

Friends pretend to be interested
when you analyze your dreams.

❧

Discussing baby names with a
friend is so much more productive
than with your spouse (who has
his heart set on "Brewster").

A tennis partner.

∽

You could take swing
dancing together.

∽

Who better to be your egg donor?

∽

Nobody will know the difference if
you borrow her library card.

Someone to sit with on
the Ferris wheel.

∽

A friend will send you postcards
from exotic vacation spots.

∽

She *wants* to see your
tummy-tuck scars.

∽

If your picture's in the paper, a
friend will send you a copy.

How to Recognize That a Friendship Is Over

∽

He returns the videocassette of *Sister Act* that he borrowed from you in 1995.

∽

No more vacation postcards.

Instead of biweekly phone calls,
you receive a universal Christmas
letter in the mail.

∽

Your other friends have
already split up into two camps:
yours and hers.

∽

Your mothers no longer speak
when they bump into each other
at church or the Safeway.

He finally admits he thinks
this cast of *Saturday Night Live*
is the best one yet.

෴

You hate her for using the verb
"to party" in every sentence.

෴

You hate him for labeling
his hard-boiled eggs in
the refrigerator.

She intentionally
overwaters your African
violet when you go away
for the weekend.

∽

At a party, the only
time she talks to you is
when she's waiting for
the bathroom, too.

She doesn't call to ask
you what you're going
to wear tonight.

∽

She puts sugar in your coffee
instead of Sweet 'n' Low.

Will dress up as Santa and visit
your kids on Christmas Eve.

◡

Someone to drive you home after
you've had your wisdom teeth out.

◡

Someone to pledge a sorority with.

◡

At least one person out there
likes you enough to send
you a Valentine.

A real friend won't get mad when you forget her birthday.

～

Someone who will cheerfully (or at least silently) wear the hideous bridesmaid's dresses you've chosen for your wedding.

～

He can drop the lobster into the pot for you.

It's much less embarrassing to make a late-night call to your friend than to the radio call-in show.

ॐ

Thanksgiving with friends is much more fun than Thanksgiving with your family.

ॐ

A friend will cover for you when your mom calls wondering where you are.

Once in a while,
you can unload a spare cat
on a friend.

❦

Inventing secret
codes together.

❦

Someone who thinks you
could still wear your cheerleading
skirt if you had to.

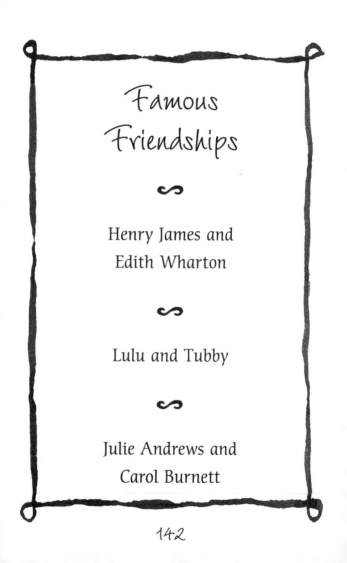

Famous
Friendships

⌇

Henry James and
Edith Wharton

⌇

Lulu and Tubby

⌇

Julie Andrews and
Carol Burnett

Don Rickles and
Bob Newhart

∽

Gertrude Stein and
Pablo Picasso

∽

Tom Hanks and
Steven Spielberg

∽

Richard Gere and
the Dalai Lama

Suzanne Somers and
her Thighmaster

✂

Robert Redford and
Paul Newman

✂

Jack Nicholson and
Warren Beatty

✂

God and the Pope

Richard Rodgers and
Oscar Hammerstein

Jocelyn Wildenstein and
her plastic surgeon

All the ex-wives of John Derek

Donald Trump and
his publicist

Kathi Lee and Kathi Lee

∽

Diane von Furstenburg
and Barry Diller

∽

Rocky and Bullwinkle

∽

Naomi Campbell and
Nelson Mandela

∽

Miss Daisy and her chauffeur

She won't remind you
about the time you booted on
Chip Jenson's feet.

∽

Shh! A lot of your friends hate
The Velveteen Rabbit, too.

∽

They'll explain the birds and
the bees to your kids.

Who better to con into taking
drawing classes with you?

∽

If the parents say it's okay,
you can bring a friend along
when you're babysitting.

∽

You can each subscribe to
a different magazine and then
trade them mid-month. Not
that you'll ever remember.

Someone to get birth control
with that first time.

❧

Male friends don't think
disgusting, disgusting cigars
are disgusting at all.

❧

A good friend is unlikely to come
up behind you and, shrieking,
bury a hatchet in your back.

A friend with kids can keep you "hep" to the latest slang.

∽

A friend in the entertainment business can keep you up-to-date on George Clooney's activities.

∽

Someone to give you your insulin shot.

You've always got at least
one friend whose parents are
even worse than yours.

༄

Borrow his notes when you
sleep through Spanish 101.

༄

She doesn't think you're
a baby for crying.

Not-So-Famous
Friendships

∾

Harpo Marx and
Robert Benchley

∾

Unity Mitford and Hitler

∾

Truman Capote and that
former wife of Johnny Carson

Carrie Fisher and
Penny Marshall

∾

Betsy, Tacy, and Tib

∾

Steve Martin and
Martin Short

∾

Marky Post and
President Clinton

Burt Reynolds and
Dom DeLuise

∽

Carol Matthau, Oona Chaplin,
and Gloria Vanderbilt

∽

Wally Cox and Marlon Brando

∽

Nancy Drew and
Hannah Gruen

Katharine Graham's mother
and Thomas Mann

ᔐ

Whitey and Lumpy

ᔐ

Michael Keaton and
Barry Bonds

ᔐ

Henry Kissinger and
Jill St. John

Lady Elaine Fairchild
and that cat

∽

Willie Nelson and
Jimmy Carter

∽

Barbra Streisand and
President Clinton's mother

Somewhere out there is someone
you can befriend who knows how
to hang wallpaper.

∽

Someone to keep you company
in the gift-wrap line.

∽

Only a friend would help you hem
a skirt with chewed-up gum. Your
mother wouldn't dream of it.

You don't mind if a friend
sees you throwing up.

∽

You can trade babysitting
with a friend whose kids are
the same age as yours.

∽

Someone to cut off that
forbidden swatch of carpet
at the decorating store.

You don't have to raise
your child's allowance until
your friends raise *their*
children's allowances.

∽

She doesn't think you're
crazy for buying an Aga.

∽

A friend will let you drink
soda with your dinner.

Someone who will go
out of her way to give
you a lift home.

༄

Someone to take a
wine-tasting course with.

༄

You can wear your shirt
untucked around a friend.

Without your best friend,
you'd never dare go back to
high school reunions.

☙

A friend can be your labor coach,
even though it *is* kind of sad.

☙

Someone who will—without being
told—find the larger size for you
on the rack because she knew the
6 would never ever fit, but didn't
want to have to tell you so herself.

Why Animal Friends Are Better Than People Friends

∽

Cheaper to buy
presents for

∽

Willingness to fetch

Don't know the difference
between leftovers and
same-day cooking

Never complain about their
love life or their children

Never borrow money

Can be kept on an actual leash,
not just an emotional one

Don't care if you remember
their birthdays

∽

The perfect houseguest:
they'll sleep outside

∽

Don't get embarrassed when
you vacuum the sofa after
they've been sitting on it

Won't notice if you
accidentally call them by
your child's name

∽

Don't get bored just sitting
there watching you

∽

Wear tags so you don't have
to worry so much about their
getting lost forever

Bark when a burglar breaks
into your house, instead of
cowering in the closet

∾

Will jump into the water
and pull you out with their teeth
(does not work for cats)

A friend won't tell the historic commission that you replaced your wooden shutters with vinyl ones.

∾

It was so, so hilarious that time she mooned Mr. Francis!

∾

If you're both guys, you can play all eighteen holes without saying a word.

Someone to get caught
shoplifting with.

∽

Quick! Befriend the office bully
and no one will pick on you.

∽

Look, there's nothing *wrong* with
having a friend who belongs to the
most exclusive club in town.

It's easier to crash a
party with a friend.

❧

A friend won't try to
wrestle custody of your
kids away from you.

❧

Friends don't worry
that raw cookie dough might
give them salmonella.

Well-intentioned, and armed with
a pair of tweezers . . .

ა

When you give a speech, a friend
will laugh in the right places.

ა

Maybe your best friend's
husband will console you when
he discovers that your husband
is in love with his wife.

The Do's, Don'ts, and Do Not's of Slumber Parties

∾

Do not invite someone who keeps saying, "Come on, guys. Isn't it time to get some shut-eye?"

∾

Do not plan on doing anything important the next day, like starring in your soccer game or playing in your piano recital.

Don't go if you
don't like pizza.

&

Make sure to lay in a good
supply of Mad Libs.

&

Never laugh during the séance.

&

Two words: (1) junk
and (2) food.

Don't bother playing that trick
where you dip someone's hand
in warm water: it never works,
and you always spill the water.
The shaving-cream trick usually
works okay, though.

∽

Bring your
own pillow.

Make *sure* you know
whether the other kids will
be sleeping in pajamas,
nightgowns, or the clothes
they were already wearing.

∽

Move all the birthday
presents out of the way
before you spread out
your sleeping bags.

Don't have the "slumber" part of
the party out in the yard. Even
though no one ever falls asleep
anyway, grass is way too
uncomfortable to sleep on.

Plan on everyone being
in tears at some point.

Plan on everyone saying
"You know what? I really, really
hate you!" at some point.

Remember that the same person
who keeps wanting everyone
to get some shut-eye will also
be the same person who tries
to wake everyone up early the
next morning. Again, do
not invite this person.

∽

Screaming during the ghost
stories is a good way to make
the next-door neighbors
call the police.

A ghost-story-teller is always
lying when s/he says s/he knows
the person the ghost story
happened to. Nor does s/he
know the "friend of a friend"
it happened to.

∽

You do not have to pay
attention when the host's
parents come down and yell
at you. At least not the
first three times.

It is not your host's/hostess's
fault if his/her younger sibling
gets to join the party. It's the
parents' fault. Blame them.

∽

Don't leave the snacks on the
floor if your host owns a dog.

∽

Even though your parents say
they won't mind if you call them
at three A.M. and want a ride
home, they *will* mind.

Okay, it's kind of lame—but you can buy a friend one of those "Thinking of You" cards.

∽

Someone who cares as much as you do about the Miller sisters.

∽

Friends are happy when you cook them a bad meal. It takes the pressure off the next time you come to *their* house.

You can hang up on a friend's
machine without fear of
being star-69'd.

∾

Last year you directed the
Christmas pageant. This year,
by God, it's *her* turn.

∾

A friend shouldn't get exasperated
when you ask to borrow a pen.

Less likely to sue if they slip
on your front steps.

∾

Less scary than a spouse to argue
with, and with fewer consequences.

∾

You can split the cost of power
tools neither of you use very often.

∾

Likewise, the cost of ladders.

Endless games of
I Doubt It and Snap.

ⸯ

The thrill of taking a
blood vow together.

ⸯ

Someone to empty the
mousetrap for you.

ⸯ

Go ahead! Sign up for the
decorating committee together.

Someone to protect you from having to talk to Hare Krishna recruiters at airports.

ꚸ

She won't laugh at you for caring about the paternity of Princess Stephanie's youngest child.

ꚸ

At least one of your friends believes you're a genius.

ꚸ

"Jinx! You owe me a Coke!"

Above and Beyond the Call of Friendship: Things You Should Not Ask a Friend to Do

❦

Change your baby's
poopy diaper

❦

Join your cult

Be the photographer
at your wedding

Check the bottom
of your foot to see
whether it's a callus
or a plantar wart

Give you a
chemical peel

Give you a tattoo

∽

Return a dented can of
soup to the A&P

∽

Be a surrogate mother

∽

Read your father's novel

Bathe your cat

∽

Lend you his oxygen mask
on the plane

∽

Come to your one-year-old's
birthday party

∽

Get rid of an old
mattress for you

Cut your toenails

❧

Take your kids to see
Santa at Macy's on the day
after Thanksgiving

❧

Steal you a bathrobe
from a fancy hotel

❧

Fix you up with someone

Pee in a cup for you if you
have a drug problem

∽

Take your family's
Christmas-card picture

∽

Smuggle cigars
through customs for
your husband

"Miss Lucy had a baby/She
named him Tiny Tim . . ."

&

Friends make more interesting
godparents than relatives do.

&

Without friends, your aunt
would have to be maid of honor
at your wedding.

Someone who can debate
shaving/waxing/Nair until
you're *sure* about your favorite
method of depilatory.

೧

Friends can save seats
for each other.

೧

She'll never remind you
that you left the sugar out of
your banana bread.

He won't tell Miss Wellman
that you were the one who put
the glue on her chair.

❧

A buddy to shop with at a sample
sale; one of you shops while the
other waits in the long checkout
line, and then you switch.

❧

Doesn't understand your love of
bologna sandwiches, but doesn't
tease you about it either.

When everyone else has
stopped coming to your
annual Fourth of July picnic,
a friend will still come.

❧

Remembers when you
loved Peter Frampton.

❧

Will hold your hand for
the entire flight.

Unfun Activities That Become Fun with a Friend

∽

Watching a Demi Moore movie

∽

Getting lost

∽

Spending the night in
a fleabag hotel

Jogging

∽

Going to the gym

∽

Going to the
unemployment office

∽

Giving blood

Being caught in
a downpour

❦

Waiting in line

❦

Mucking out a stable

❦

House-painting

Cleaning the kitchen

∽

Clipping the
dog's toenails

∽

Writing a book

∽

Commuting

Watching cricket

❧

Shopping for mothballs

❧

Driver's ed

❧

Jury duty

❧

Working at the polling booth

Being a Brownie leader

∽

Putting up a new shower curtain

∽

Deciding what should go
to the thrift shop

∽

Planting bulbs

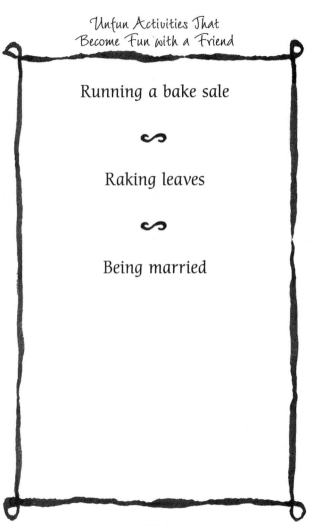

Running a bake sale

〜

Raking leaves

〜

Being married

Who are you going to tell dirty
jokes to—your mother?

∽

Jumping rope and playing jacks.

∽

When all else fails, a friend
will help you fill in the rest
of a sentence that begins
"When all else fails."

Phony phone calls.

༄

"Teddy bear, teddy bear, turn
around . . . "

༄

If your friend is president
of the PTA, you don't have
to go to meetings.

If your friend is president
of the USA, you can sleep
in the Lincoln Bedroom.

∽

Someone to say "Steady,
steady . . ." when you're cutting
down a tree with your chain saw.

∽

Maybe he won't tell his wife
you're the one who broke
the margarita pitcher.

How else are you going to
learn the facts of life?

∾

Someone to call from
the bathroom during
your blind date.

∾

Playing tennis with a friend
who's better than you are
will improve your game.

How to Turn an Ex-Lover into a Friend

∽

Find him someone else.

∽

Pretend you're a good sport.

∽

Keep up with his parents.

Attend his sister's wedding.

∽

Listen endlessly to the details
of his new courtship.

∽

Give the *new* happy couple
a wedding shower.

∽

Befriend the new lover.

Wear a skort to show that you don't care how he sees you dress anymore. (Note: This also works for turning a current lover into a friend.)

ᔑ

Offer to babysit his dog.

ᔑ

Water the happy couple's plants while they're on their honeymoon.

Help him pick out her
engagement ring.

Help his new girlfriend
buy him his Valentine's
Day boxers.

Pass along all your
unused condoms.

Help her move into his
apartment.

∽

Buy her an engagement
present with her new
initials on it.

∽

Start dating Matt Damon.

Playing tennis with a friend
who's worse than you are will
teach you patience.

∽

Doing chores at a friend's house
always seems more interesting
than doing them at home.

∽

Turning your basement into a haunted
house at Halloween is a great way
to discover neighborhood friends
you never knew you had.

If you're too drunk to drive, hand over your keys to a sober friend.

෴

Someone to whom you can say, "I'm sorry, but I *never* go to brunch."

෴

"What's thine is mine."

෴

For males, it is not a sign of dislike to punch a friend.

Remembers when you
decorated your room in Day-Glo
posters and black lights.

❦

Endless games of
Chinese jump rope.

❦

"Thou shalt not covet" doesn't
apply to your friends' stuff.

A friend remembers all the words
to your old sorority songs.

∽

A friend may not exactly come to
your rescue when the big kids are
teasing you, but he will at least
stand silent nearby.

∽

Learn chess together,
and forget it together.

Remembers when you
decorated your bedroom in
Leif Garrett posters.

∽

Anyone at the ice-skating rink
who has a skate key automatically
counts as a friend.

∽

Travel with a friend and
you don't have to sit next to
a stranger on the plane.

"Come-Off Lines:" How Not to Start a Friendship

❧

Can I borrow a thousand dollars?

❧

I don't have any friends—do you?

❧

Is this yours? I found it
in the bathroom.

I can't seem to get rid
of this cold.

ꙅ

Do you like me yet?

ꙅ

I just know angels are watching
over us right now.

ꙅ

So! How do you think the
friendship's going so far?

Smell my breath. Is it bad?

❧

Can you believe I used
to be a man?

❧

I just got into the worst fight
with my best friend.

❧

Hey, do you mind if I ask
you an enormous favor?

May I be blunt?

∽

What did you get on your SATs?

∽

I just bought my first
Powerball ticket. You wanna
know my numbers?

∽

Have you accepted Jesus as
your personal savior?

Don't turn around.
I think that man over there
works for the CIA.

∽

Can you see if my contact
lens is in my eye?

∽

Everything sucks these days.
Agreed?

∽

Is this seat saved?

What smells?

&

I'm a recent grad of
a CPR course!

&

My name is Tony,
and I'm an alcoholic.

&

Do you light
Sabbath candles?

My therapist said something
really interesting today.

∽

Can I use your comb?

∽

Did you happen to catch
Leno the other night?

∽

Is this a lymph node?

Have you read the
Book of Mormon yet?

ಌ

Which is your favorite Teletubby?

ಌ

I don't care what they say.
Common courtesy has *not* gone
out of fashion.

ಌ

Are you the person in the
household who makes the
long-distance decisions?

Cheaper calls if you sign up for the
Friends and Family program.

∽

When a friend comes over
for dinner, you don't have to
put out nuts or hors d'oeuvres
. . . or napkins.

∽

Friends trust you with
their spouses.

If your friend and her spouse die,
you get their children . . . *and* all
the insurance money.

భ

You can tear up unabashedly
in front of a friend when the
national anthem is sung.

భ

A friend will tell the host you were
there when you weren't.

A friend won't tell anyone
you color your hair.

∾

A friend never makes you feel
guilty about taking her last stick
of gum. She chews it herself.

∾

When a friend calls too early in
the morning, you don't have to
say you were already up.

A friend knows all your stories, in case you forget the punch line.

∽

Someone to fill you in on what you missed in the movie while you were at the concession stand.

∽

Someone who will lend you their photogenic child or dog for *your* vanity Christmas card photo.

With Friends Like These . . .

∽

Brutus

∽

Linda Tripp

∽

Iago

With Friends Like These . . .

Judas

৵

Benedict Arnold

৵

Paul Theroux

৵

Julia Phillips

৵

Clarence Thomas

Pete Rose

∽

George Steinbrenner

∽

Becky Sharp

∽

Undine Spragg

∽

Rasputin

O.J. Simpson

∽

Martha Stewart

∽

Cousine Bette

∽

Reverend Arthur Dimsdale

∽

Uriah Heep

Nellie Olson

ৎ

Tonya Harding

ৎ

Cotton Mather

A friend won't think less of
you for secretly loving *The Bridges
of Madison County.*

ᔕ

A friend won't think less of you
for having read only the Cliffs
Notes to *Twelfth Night.*

ᔕ

A friend won't think less of
you for not voting.

Hopscotch (for about eight minutes).

❧

A friend remembers the names of
everyone in your extended family,
and asks after them once in a while.

❧

A friend lets you watch TV
during dinner.

❧

Well, at least friendly fire is better
than the other kind.

You'll never have to go to a scary
doctor's appointment alone.

∽

A friend will stop splashing you in
the pool as soon as you say stop.

∽

Someone to split entrées
with at a restaurant.

∽

Help yourself. You don't have to ask
which drawer the silverware is in.

Without friends, who'd fill up
your autograph book?

∽

You don't have to keep pictures of
your friends in your wallet.

∽

A friend might give you his theater
tickets if he's sick. (P.S. Though the
friend couldn't have known, it somehow
always turns out that the understudy is
standing in for the main character.)

You can *force* a friend of the opposite
sex to take you to your senior prom
if you don't have a date.

ॐ

If a friend makes you a casserole,
she puts it in a foil pan rather
than something you have
to wash and return.

ॐ

A Dolce & Gabbana-wearing
friend can get you
past the bouncer.

238

Synonyms for
Friend

∽

Pal

∽

Colleague

∽

Peer

Companion

Close acquaintance

Amigo

Chum

Patron

∽

Playmate

∽

Well-wisher

∽

Confidante

Accomplice

∽

Ally

∽

Enabler

∽

Codependent

A good book

§

TV

§

Candy

§

Microwave popcorn

Unlike a spouse, a friend will not
say "You missed a spot" while
watching you vacuum.

છે

A spouse may complain if you spend
a night on the town with a friend.
A friend will not complain if you spend
a night on the town with your spouse.

છે

You're not going to send a chain
letter to your minister, are you?

It's not bad luck to throw
away a chain letter sent to
you by a friend.

∽

Someone with whom you can trust
your online password.

∽

Having a friend who cheats
on his/her spouse lets you feel
like a better spouse.

Before you go to the doctor, your friend will convince you it's nothing, no matter what your medical symptom.

❦

You never have to go to the ladies' room in a restaurant alone.

❦

Someone to keep you company when all the women at your table go off to the bathroom.

Without friends, you'd have to
hire extras to be your bridesmaids.

ᔐ

Someone to be your
Buddy during hikes
at summer camp.

ᔐ

You can send a friend
newspaper clippings without
enclosing a cover letter.

"What's Great
About Your Best
Friend?"
— Kids Tell Us

∽

"He has Nintendo 64 and
PlayStation."

∽

"Better snacks at their house."

"When you sleep over at
Dawne's house, you can
stay up *way* late."

"Mine has a summer bedroom
and a winter bedroom."

"His father lets us drive up and
down the driveway."

"Trampoline."

"She doesn't press too hard
when we're coloring."

∽

"The Clarks don't make you
balance your meals."

∽

"Mara's mother designs
for Esprit."

∽

"Satellite dish."

"Ian's father invents
video games."

∽

"Max's dad is in a band."

∽

"She has a magic wand."

∽

"She has My Size Barbie."

∽

"His dad once shot an elk!"

"She's a great artist."

ᔄ

"He's really great at
building Lego."

ᔄ

"Piles of old Playboys."

ᔄ

"There's a clubhouse in
his crawl space."

"He hasn't brushed his teeth
in six months."

❧

"Rachel doesn't even have
to wear shoes. *Her* parents
carry her everywhere."

❧

"Great skateboarder—he gets
in lots of accidents."

❧

"She's popular."

"His dad coaches something
every season."

∽

"Her parents let us
watch R movies."

∽

"She's allowed to
hate her sister."

Someone to send cheesy books
about friendship to.

∽

Getting to sit next to your
friends on the bus makes up
for the boringness of that field
trip to the Town Hall.

∽

A really good friend is
a reliable film critic.

Friends are nicer than family
when it comes to putting up
with your little phases.

෴

If a friend forwards you
something from the Internet,
there's at least a semi-good chance
that it will be worth reading.

෴

They let you butt in front
of them in line.

A friend doesn't make you
clean your room.

∽

She understands the appeal
of Filene's Basement.

∽

Without friends, friendships
are just ships.

∽

Someone to talk to at
Coffee Hour after church.

257

You know what it's okay
to tease each other about,
and what it's not.

∽

You don't mind letting them
see you in the cruddy old sweats
that pass for your pj's.

∽

Someone to help you across the
street (if you happen to be old,
and if you happen to consider
Boy Scouts "friends").

Being Friends with the Famous: A Caveat

∽

Never call the paparazzi before you go out to dinner.

∽

Never ask for their autograph.

Don't tell them about
your screenplay.

❧

Do not confuse the bald
ones or the Baldwins.

❧

Never bring a camera to
Thanksgiving dinner.

❧

Never ask, "What's Michael
Jordan *really* like?"

Don't make restaurant
reservations in their name
unless they're joining
you for dinner.

∽

Always love their
latest novel.

∽

Watch them on
Charlie Rose.

At a party, never assume people
are interested in you.

❧

Never volunteer them for your
child's school benefit.

❧

Don't drag over lesser friends
to be introduced to them.

❧

Don't assume they mean it
when they say, "I'd love to."

Never ask, "Where do you get your ideas?"

ꕔ

Don't tell anyone you know them.

ꕔ

When they give you their publicist's phone number, the friendship is over.

Friends can remain on the
phone in silence while watching
the same TV program.

ᔣ

Okay, she remembers every
embarrassing thing you've ever
done . . . but she's unlikely
to blackmail you.

ᔣ

Friends who like gardening are
happy to fill your planters.

Friends with large estates are
happy to let you cut down your
Christmas tree on their property.

෨

A real friend will not
steal your nanny.

෨

If you accidentally spit while talking
to a friend, you don't have to kill
yourself as much as you would if
it had happened while you were
talking to someone important.

A friend will discuss ad
nauseam what you should wear
on an upcoming date.

∾

You can make million-dollar
bets with a friend without
consequences.

∾

A friend won't tell anyone if you
go to the museum gift shop
instead of the exhibit.

Without friends, there would be
no good wedding toasts.

❧

Friends never accuse you of being
politically incorrect.

❧

A friend won't put a V-chip in your TV.

❧

You can make a friend call you to test
out your new answering machine.

A friend doesn't care if you eat
your vegetables.

∾

A friend can't force you to
go to bed on time.

∾

A friend doesn't make you
take piano lessons.

Great Places to Find Friends

∽

at church

∽

doing volunteer work

∽

at your kids' play groups

∽

in line at the grocery store

in adult education classes

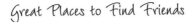

at Lamaze classes

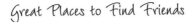

on guided tours
of foreign countries

at impromptu performances
of Handel's *Messiah*

in the seat next to you
when you have season
tickets for the opera

❧

at yoga

❧

in community
theater groups

❧

online

Boring board games are not quite as boring when you play them at a friend's house.

∽

A *real* friend never forgets his wallet when you go out for dinner.

∽

A friend gives your kids her kids' hand-me-downs.

A parakeet in the house means you'll always have someone to say your name over and over.

ↄ

A friend will help with the guests' coats at your party.

ↄ

Someone to join your rotisserie league.

Someone to take a CPR
class with.

∾

Who else is going to give you
dentist/doctor/accountant
recommendations?

∾

Someone to watch your
luggage at the airport while you
go to the bathroom.

Someone to grow old with.

∽

Your friend likes your betrothed, loves your spouse, hates your ex, then re-appreciates him/her when you get back together.

∽

A friend never has enough bad things to say about someone you don't like.

Not-So-Great Places to Find Friends

∽

under a cabbage leaf

∽

"the stork brings them"

∽

stuck in your chimney
on Christmas Eve

prying up a manhole
and peeking in

ᔪ

getting stuck in the
elevator together

ᔪ

in the emergency room

ᔪ

when you rear-end
their car

when your house gets
picked up in a tornado
and dropped down on
their fellow witch

ა

in the dentist's chair

ა

small claims court

at Filene's Basement

∽

during your
parent-teacher
conference

∽

at singles' bars

at the only
parking space in
the whole mall

∽

weighing your packages
at the post office on the
day before Christmas

∽

online

Someone who'll pick you
first or second for the team,
even though you're not that
great a volleyball player.

ॐ

Someone to use as an emergency
phone number at the kids' schools
and camps because you actually
like her more than your sister.

ॐ

Someone to push you
on the swing.

281

Someone who doesn't belittle
you for caring that you have
a *real* Gucci bag.

ço

Someone who pretends she doesn't
notice your "Gucci" bag was
manufactured in the Ivory Coast.

ço

A friend's presentable sibling
can always be pressed into
service as your date.

She knows how many times
a week you go to the shrink,
and could care less.

∽

Someone who won't laugh at
you when you fantasize about
running away to Tuscany.

∽

He swears that in a certain pose
you look just like Candice Bergen.

When you say, "Sometimes I just think I should run for office," your friend laughs far less zestfully than your wife or husband does.

∽

An eye to catch when your boss says something stupid.

∽

She doesn't expect you to be peppy.

A friend will come over and
help you get rid of extra
clothes in your closet.

∽

Friends can call each other
when they have absolutely
nothing to say.

∽

Share a friend's drink
without fear of germs.

A Friend Always Has . . .

∽

a better-looking trainer

∽

a more honest contractor

∽

the *best* pediatrician

a better-trained masseuse

∽

a sager grandfather

∽

a wilier accountant

∽

a more prescient psychic

∽

the most infallible
hangover remedy

a meaner divorce lawyer

∽

a more fabulous
hairdresser

∽

a richer godmother

∽

a better-connected
real estate broker

a subtler colorist

~

a more available
babysitter

~

a cheaper tailor

~

a funnier uncle

better-behaved kids

❦

a more interesting book club

❦

a younger girlfriend

❦

a more powerful juice machine

❦

a personal shopper

Friends don't care if you
wear the same thing two days
in a row. If they are male,
they don't even notice.

જ

Friends never trip you
on purpose.

જ

A friend may throw a snowball
at you, but the snowball will
not have a rock in it.

A friend can't make you call
Aunt Frieda on her birthday.

❦

The most fun activity on earth:
looking through your old
yearbooks with your old friends
from high school.

❦

A friend believes you
when you say you were
stuck in traffic.

292

Someone to talk about the
party with after it's over.

∽

You can ask a friend really
rudimentary grammar questions
without shame.

∽

In a court of law,
friends will fudge the truth
in your favor.

Someday, you and a group of friends can rent a sailboat and cruise the Caribbean.

❧

You can wash dishes while you talk on the phone to a friend.

❧

A friend will organize the neighbors to cook for your family if your spouse is in the hospital.

What You Can Learn
from Friends

∽

If you have two best friends
instead of one, the three
of you always have something
to talk about.

∽

You can survive even
when someone you like is
mad at you.

In every friendship,
no matter how close, certain
topics should be avoided.

❦

Even local calls add up.

❦

It's possible to hem a skirt
with earring studs.

❦

Pecking orders are not
just for birds.

People who are nowhere
near your age can still
be worth knowing.

∽

Friends can like you without
having to invite you to every
party they give.

∽

A burden shared is
a burden halved.

Even so, "I'm here if you
need me" does not mean
"on and on into infinity."

Everyone comes from a
dysfunctional family.

It's much more fun to
break a diet if you have
someone to do it with.

Contrary to what you thought in college, it *is* possible to like someone whose politics are different from yours.

∽

There are many, many views on what constitutes a pretty Christmas tree.

A friend who is doing you
a favor will not appreciate
"helpful" suggestions about
the best way to do it.

❦

Sometimes a glass of
wine is the best
companion on earth.

❦

A friend can criticize his/her
mother, but you can't.

How to arrange the furniture
in your living room.

∽

The other couple in your
car pool are having
marital problems.

∽

Never venture to give
advice unless it is asked for.
Even then, be careful.

She won't tell anyone it's your
child who has the head lice.

∽

Your friends can be trusted not
to tell your child the truth
about Santa Claus—unlike
the child's friends.

∽

A friend won't cheat you
in a coin toss.

For a long time, you can force your kids to be friends with your friends' kids.

You can serve a friend instant coffee and tea-bag tea.

Someone to prompt you when you blow your lines in the glee club play.

Friends never keep track
of who calls whom.

&

Friends never have to
waste time catching up.

&

A friend won't ask if you've
done your homework.

&

A friend can fall asleep while
talking to you on the phone.

A friend can hang up on
you for another call.

∽

"Make new friends but
keep the old/One is silver
and the other's gold."

∽

A friend doesn't care if you
get a C in biology.

A friend will laugh at
your terrible Jack Nicholson
impression.

Their parents sometimes have
great old comedy LPs.

Remember that summer the two of
you read *The Outsiders*?

Great Things about NBC's "Friends"

You get to watch Joey's
weight fluctuate.

What's the deal with
Monica's hair? It looks
horrible this season.

That little frame the girls put up around the peephole in their door—great decorating idea!

ↄ

Central Perk is never crowded.

ↄ

It's funny how Chandler and Joey can forget about the duck and the chicken for weeks at a time—and yet both birds continue to flourish.

There will never be another
actor who does the
sad-puppy look as well as
David Schwimmer.

∽

Semi-steady employment
for Elliott Gould.

∽

The way they title the shows
"The One Where . . ."

Any time any of the characters
start dating anyone who's
not a main character,
you know it won't last.

A friend cannot be reformatted
to fit your screen.

❧

If a friend finds God,
she will not demand
that you follow suit.

❧

Don't worry. None of your friends
has read Proust either.

Once in a while, a friend
can trim your bangs.

❧

Friends don't laugh at you for
being afraid of the dentist.

❧

A friend will never
give you one of those
"Over the Hill" coffee
mugs for your birthday.

A friend understands that
when you visit, of course the cat
has to stay in the bedroom.

∽

A friend understands
that of course the well-being
of your cat comes first.

∽

A friend will listen to your
boring cute pet stories.

She'll tuck the tag back
into your collar.

∽

Listen, she owes you one.

∽

Friends just, you know, *get* it.